I CAN'T STOP CRYING

I CAN'T STOP CRYING

GRIEF AND RECOVERY
A Compassionate Guide

JOHN D. MARTIN
AND FRANK D. FERRIS, MD
FOREWORD BY ROBERT BUCKMAN, MD, PhD

McClelland & Stewart

First published by Key Porter Books in 1992
McClelland & Stewart edition published in 2013

Library and Archives Canada Cataloguing in Publication

Martin, John D.
    I can't stop crying : grief and recovery, a compassionate guide / John D. Martin and Frank D. Ferris.

ISBN 978-0-7710-5461-7

    1. Bereavement – Psychological aspects. 2. Death – Psychological aspects. 3. Grief. I. Ferris, Frank D. II. Title.

BF575.G7M215 2013   155.9'37   C2012-903905-5

Typeset in Electra by M&S, Toronto
Printed and bound in the United States of America

McClelland & Stewart,
a division of Random House of Canada Limited
One Toronto Street, Suite 300
Toronto, ON
M5C 2V6
www.mcclelland.com

1   2   3   4   5   17   16   15   14   13

To Constance and Christopher:

With your love, support, and encouragement, this book, and all the things that brought it together, were possible.

After the death of his wife,
C. S. Lewis wrote of his grief:

*"I'm not afraid, but no one told me it
would feel so much like fear."*

Contents

Foreword

For a variety of reasons, our society has lost touch with the process of understanding and accepting death and grief. As a result, we seem to have difficulty grieving in a normal and healthy way. In this book, the authors address that lack, offering perspective to the person who is grieving. They explain and document the different components of and reactions in the grief response, to create a coherent and sensible picture of what is often a bewildering and confusing time.

Using the three Rs – realize, recognize, and rebuild – this book emphasizes the often-forgotten point that grief, however painful, has a purpose and an objective: to allow us to reconstruct our lives after a major loss. In addition, this book underlines the differences between healthy and unhealthy grief reactions. Using their own experiences as grief therapists, the authors offer practical advice, shedding light on a topic that is clouded by misunderstanding.

I Can't Stop Crying can and should be read by anyone going through grief, and perhaps by everyone else as well. Our society needs to be re-educated in understanding grief. This book is part of that much-needed enlightenment.

Dr. Robert Buckman, MD, PhD (1992)

Preface

If you have ever experienced the death of someone close to you, such as your spouse or partner, or a close friend, you will remember just how different you felt after his or her death. Whether the death occurred recently or several years ago, you may still be feeling very different. These feelings are often overwhelming and so personal that other people seem to have great difficulty understanding them.

In our daily work, we see many people who have experienced the death of someone close to them, or the loss of something significant to them. Throughout this book, these people – the true experts – will speak to you about their feelings, struggles, and situations. Through their experiences, we hope you will see that you are not as alone as you might think. We will also suggest ways that might help you cope with your loss and feelings.

Most often, the grief that we see is in response to the death of a partner. We use the term *partner* or *loved one* to refer to all of the important relationships (e.g., spouses, common-law and gay/lesbian partners, lovers, parents, siblings, intimate friends, and companions) that people share in life.

This book will speak mostly about the grief associated with the loss of a partner. However, we believe that the issues we present can easily be applied to the grief associated with any death, or to any situation where there has been a significant loss.

We have heard all of the stories in this book many times. Any resemblance to a real person is only coincidental.

Although this book is the result of collaboration between two authors, for simplicity we shall speak as one voice.

In 2011, Robert Buckman, who was influential in the writing of this book and encouraging in many ways, died suddenly. He was a strong supporter, and we continue to feel grateful for his help.

In addition, we would like to give thanks to those who contributed significantly to making this work possible: Helen McNeal, Reverend Alan Tipping, Heidi Winter, and especially Barbara Durette.

Thank you also to Kendra Ward, and to McClelland & Stewart and Random House of Canada.

Introduction

When *I Can't Stop Crying* was originally published more than twenty years ago, I knew that permission was an essential tool for recovering from grief. I understood by experience and somehow by instinct, that those who had suffered loss through the death of a loved one needed, perhaps more than anything else, to be able to feel, say, and do what they must in order to begin to recover from their pain.

Responding to grief can be very difficult. The death of one person will have ripples that will touch the lives of many. Sometimes it's clear to see who the griever is, to identify who needs our support and attention. But at other times things can become very confusing. Dad dies and so Mom is the primary griever. However, if there are children, they too are hurting, maybe at very different levels and at different times. Grandchildren, if there are any, will have feelings of grief, and siblings of the person who has died may be having trouble. Surely friends, and possibly co-workers, of the one gone will also be touched by the loss. Our roles are not clear-cut. Today, you may be the one in need; tomorrow, the one helping to care for a family member or friend, who may need help too. Because grief has so many changing dynamics and since the needs of those who are hurting around us are often shifting, we have difficulty knowing what to say or what to do. So, unfortunately, we often say and do things that cause the person who is hurting more pain. We don't want to say something that might cause more discomfort. We try hard to speak of pleasantries and daily life, all the while hoping desperately that the one grieving doesn't really need our help. What would we do then?

But a cliché here, a bit of patronization there, all in the name of not knowing what to say, often makes the whole thing worse. We avoid what needs to be spoken of, or at least offered. None of this is difficult to understand, but often adds to the feeling that expressions of grief are somehow "wrong," or to be done only in private.

Over the years I have come to believe even more firmly in the power of permission to heal. Being able to find and receive permission to grieve allows the process of grief to begin and enables those who are hurting to feel and express themselves in ways that will lead to their eventual recovery.

Permission is a gift that we offer ourselves. The true act of being understood and cared for lies in our ability to be honest and authentic with our feelings and in being able to find ways to express ourselves and to tell those around us how we feel.

Permission allows us to acknowledge the hurt we feel. It provides us the courage to risk our sadness and in turn allows that our emotions are expressed and exposed to those who want to help.

Permission is also what we need to offer one another. Those we care about, our friends or family members, may feel lost, too, and at times find themselves also in need of understanding. We must try to recognize their needs and be able to say to them, "It's okay. Do what you need to. I understand that you want to help but that you hurt, too."

To those who try to help, want to help, need to help, be patient and risk being close and quiet. If you allow it, your friends who hurt will share their story with you and they will in time and with effort "feel better."

If you are grieving, lost and hurting, let others come close. Try to risk, and share your feelings. If there is no one to speak to, find another way to express how you feel – write your feelings down, paint them, scream them. It is through expression and this difficult "grief work" that we begin to heal.

Remember that society knows so little about your needs and that so much of what you experience from others may cause you frustration, confusion, and alienation.

Recovery is possible; know, however, that after you have lost a love, your perspective will never be the same. The world and everything in it will look, sound, and feel strangely different.

Whether we are grieving the death of a partner or a friend, a parent, a child, or a sibling, the reactions and inner needs of those grieving remain so similar that the basic ways to go through the grieving process apply in each situation. There are, of course, slight variations, but the suggestions and observations about how to work through the feelings will likely ring true for anyone who has experienced a significant loss.

It doesn't matter whether we speak of grief from death, divorce, retirement, children growing up and leaving home, or any other life situation that causes us sadness from its drastic change or demise; there is a process to grief that you will need to experience. In time and with very hard "work," you can recover from grief, if you take time to comprehend what has happened to you.

Acknowledging what's gone and how you've been affected is key to understanding where you are, and what you need, and to determining where and how you will go from here.

Listen to the voices in the pages that follow. They are all hurting; they are all you and me.

When you experience the loss of someone close to you, your life in all aspects will never be the same. From here you will go differently.

I Can't Stop Crying is a book for all who grieve or who have ever experienced the pain of separation from someone loved.

John Martin (2013)

I

grief

It's So Hard When Someone You Love Dies

Grief Work

Sarah Duncan called me a little over a year ago. Her name was not familiar to me, but what she told me was very familiar. I hear stories similar to hers many times over the course of a month, sometimes daily.

"You don't know me," she began, her voice shaky at best, "but I've heard of the work you do, and Dr. Johnson suggested I call you."

"What's going on, Mrs. Duncan?" I inquired.

She told me that her husband, David, had died of cancer about nine weeks earlier. She told me how lonely she felt, how alone she felt without her husband, how no one seemed to understand her feelings. She told me that life didn't seem to have any meaning for her. But most of all, she said, "I can't stop crying."

Death is the most closeted, forbidden, and frightening subject I know of. Because of the unknown, I can't, nor can anyone else, dispel the fears each of us may have about death. Although I have seen more death than I care to think about, I still can't be sure of what's beyond it. But I do know something about grief. Although we can't stop people from dying, we can do a great deal to help those who, like Sarah Duncan, can't stop crying.

To lose someone you love hurts, and it will hurt for a very long time. A major part of your life is gone, and it will never be back. It often feels like you have been robbed or cheated, or like something very significant has been ripped from you. No one can undo this hurt. Anyone who suggests to you that it's not so bad, that everything is going to be fine, that you need to focus on the good things and forget your pain, is probably too uncomfortable to really hear about your grief. It is important to find someone who will simply listen to you, and help you through these stressful times of change.

For many people, there is a common strand to the experience that follows the death of someone close. It is grief work. That is precisely what you must do. Many people feel that their pain will subside in a few weeks, or even a few months. While many claim that they are okay, I have yet to meet anyone who can truthfully and realistically cope with the death of someone close to them in much less than a year. Often it takes much longer than that.

As you read this book and work through your grief, remember three very important principles:

1. *Your feelings are subjective and unique. No one else can determine the weight or significance of your feelings.*

While others may have some idea of what you are feeling, the depth and pain of your feelings are unique to you. I have seen people in terrible pain and anguish over the death of a pet, and I have seen others who were not terribly upset over the death of a relative. While the latter situation may be rare, it does happen, and other people must never assume that they know what you are feeling.

2. *Feelings have no moral value. They are not good or bad, right or wrong; they simply exist and need to be recognized and acknowledged for what they are. How we express our feelings may have moral value, but the feelings themselves do not.*

To feel anger at a partner for dying may not seem right to some, especially if the person did not choose to die. But, if it's your feeling, it must be expressed, and heard as legitimate. By not being able to express your feelings, even the ones you believe are silly, you deny yourself the permission you need to begin to work through the emotions associated with your grief.

3. *Where your grief and the feelings that accompany it are concerned, time alone will not heal you.*

Many people will tell you that in time you will feel better. My experience tells me that is not the case. You must face your feelings and gradually work through them.

No amount of time will heal your loneliness, anger, despair, fear, or any other emotions you experience in your grief, unless you do the necessary grief work.

A broken bone will never heal properly unless it receives care and attention. Your feelings are a lot like that. Time alone may soften your hurt, but it will never help you deal with or resolve your pain.

Grief is not an illness or a disease. However, grief takes healthy and unhealthy forms, and it is often very hard to tell them apart. With guidance, you can avoid pitfalls and resolve your grief. This assistance does not have to come from an expert. It can be supplied by someone who truly understands the basic principles of grieving and will listen to you express your pain, without judgment, for as long as you need to be heard.

Take heart. You needn't cry forever!

The Heart and the Head

Sooner or Later We All Die

We know that sooner or later all of us will die. It is one of the few things we will all experience. While death is not a pleasant topic, when we are feeling well and are not facing death imminently, we can usually speak about it rationally. We know that there is a cycle to life that begins at conception. It progresses through childhood into adulthood and middle age, and, for many, on into old age. Somewhere in the cycle, death is written into the plan. We don't know when, but there is no escaping it.

For many, death is frightening because it is unknown. But death need not be an awful or ugly thing. Also, it is not necessarily tragic. It is a natural part of the life cycle that we see repeated around us every day. It is something we can plan for, speak of, educate ourselves about, and even celebrate. Death is an event that is deeply intimate and sacred for those who share in it.

With that in mind, some of the major world religions have attempted to address death not as something to be feared, but as a passage from our mortal physical existence to a spiritual one. Certainly, the concepts of "heaven," an afterlife, or re-birth see death as a transition to something new.

Of course, that's all fine if you are not facing your death or the death of someone very close to you. If you are facing a death or have recently experienced a loss, what may have seemed very reasonable or even matter-of-fact may all go out the window. This is where the heart and head can come into conflict. What seemed reasonable before may no longer make any sense at all.

Love provides us with a good analogy. When it's new, there is nothing reasonable about it. You often don't act like yourself or do the responsible thing. Your heart can cause you to do ridiculous things that your head thinks you shouldn't. New love wants to stay awake all night talking and touching, even though your head knows very well that your body needs sleep. Alas, the rest of you is paying much more attention to your heart than to your head.

Death is a lot like that. Intellectually we know that death is a part of life – a transition to another existence. All people will die. But these reasonable views get pushed aside when your heartache tells you that you're lonely, angry, lost; that you miss the person terribly and feel betrayed. All of these feelings override the intellect.

Some may suggest that these feelings aren't real. They *are* real, and very much a part of grief. While you are grieving, anything is possible. Vivian explains it like this:

> *"I couldn't think straight. I lost my keys twice, missed several appointments, turned down the wrong street on my way home, and locked myself out of the house."*

When someone you love dies, things can become very unreasonable and all the common sense in the world seems to be of little help. Your heart is hurting, and that's all you are likely to be aware of for a long time.

Permission to Do
What You Need to Do

Not so many years ago in Western culture, people were much better at coping with the death of someone close to them than we are today. Then, the cycle of life was more apparent to everyone. The family tended to be much closer. Children were born at home, and it was common for people to die at home. These events took place within the supportive structure of the whole family. Together, family members got a sense of life's coming and going.

Today, birth and death are often handled by specialists in institutions. Babies are born in high-tech delivery rooms. People frequently die in acute-care hospitals, and loved ones are sometimes not present. Mary told me:

"I spent so much time and energy looking after Neil while he was at home. When we had to admit him to hospital, the hospital staff – who were essentially strangers – took over his care and we lost all control. In the end, he even died alone as they wouldn't let us stay the night with him."

With so many people dying in institutions, many of us no longer experience the natural, full cycle of life.

Making matters worse, the strong family unit that existed in the past is, in many instances, now gone. The support that the grieving person would have been able to expect from the extended family has vanished.

Distance, from the dying and the family, makes death more frightening and unreal, and we know less about how to cope with death and the grief that follows it.

People often ask me what the key is to dealing with grief. I have come to believe that so much of coping with grief is giving yourself permission to feel the deep pain and emptiness that come with losing someone very close to you.

Jack is a young man who came to see me six months ago. His wife, Trish, had died more than a year earlier. Although he had spent time with his family doctor and two psychiatrists, he felt that he had made very little progress since her death. At the end of our third meeting, he told me something quite astonishing, something you may already have experienced:

"You are the only one who has given me permission to grieve, the only one who has said it's okay to feel sad and lonely. With you, it's okay to cry, to get angry, to go with my feelings. Everyone else told me to get on with it, to move forward and let the past be the past."

Permission is indeed the key to grieving. Without permission, you can't even get started. People sometimes don't understand that you need permission to grieve. George recounted his experience:

"Since Sue died, I can suddenly get very sad, particularly when I am out. I can't help it. I just start to cry. Often the people around me feel awkward and make me feel like I'm doing something wrong. Recently I went to visit some friends. We went out for dinner, and all of a sudden, I started to cry. My friend and his wife started fidgeting and fussing. First, they filled my wine glass. Then they started talking about things that were pleasant, and when I didn't stop crying, they said, 'What can we do for you?' 'Please just sit with me,' I said. You'd have thought I had asked for the moon. They had no idea what I was talking about, and just sat there looking confused and scared. All I wanted was for them to be close to me, and they didn't know how to do it. That's not crazy, is it?"

George's need to have his friends just sit with him is understandable. However, like so many of us, they couldn't understand, and weren't comfortable with simply doing nothing more than granting him permission to grieve.

Our society is not comfortable with granting someone permission to grieve openly. By and large, we are private people who keep things to ourselves. Even as children, we are told, "Don't yell. The neighbours will hear," or "Pull yourself together and stop crying. Do you want everyone to see that you're a mess?" But, when you're grieving, a mess is exactly what you need to be for a time, and you need to know that you have permission to be that way until you've taken the time you need to work through all of those difficult feelings. Jack recalled how others reacted to his grief:

> "Everyone kept telling me to pull myself together. 'You've got to look to the future. You've got to get on with your life.' All it did was tell me that people didn't want to hear how hurt I was, and they made me feel like I was doing something wrong."

Our society has trouble with displays of emotion. As a child I was told that boys need to be strong and that they don't cry. Boys are allowed to show aggression and, occasionally, anger; "soft emotions" are often discouraged. Girls are allowed – even expected – to cry at times, but they are considered to be whiners if they show too much weakness or emotion. Michael found such expectations to be particularly difficult:

> "I came back to work a few days after my wife's funeral. Everyone told me how terrific it was that I hadn't cried or broken down. How strong I was to get right on with things. The truth was, I wasn't eating much at all, my energy was awful, and I was crying myself to sleep every night. But, after all the undue congratulations, there was no way I could tell anyone what a mess I was inside."

Unfortunately, the permission we, like Michael, need so desperately in order to commence and continue our grieving is denied us even at our place of work. I work in a hospital. We're supposed to be sensitive to death and grief, but, if someone close to me dies, I am allowed only three days of compassionate bereavement leave! Three days – can you imagine? I understand that this is close to the standard leave permitted in many workplaces. Karen told me of her boss's reaction to her request for more time to grieve:

> "I called my boss and said I'd need another couple of days off. Do you know what he said? 'Don't be silly, you'll just sit around and mope and feel sorry for yourself. Come back to work. It will do you good!' Do me good! I could barely get out of bed."

23

The more I've seen people in trouble because they haven't been allowed to grieve, the more I've wondered whether they need a sign or symbol that notifies those around them of their situation. In North America, we seem to be getting farther and farther away from death. We don't talk about it, and when someone dies, we push those who grieve to get on with their lives as quickly as possible. By doing so, we create distance that often turns into denial, and we have no idea what denial is costing us.

Arlene told me about her wish for something to signal her pain to others:

"If only I could have let people know how much I hurt, and what a terrible state I was in. At times I wished I had a sign or a placard, something that screamed to people about the shape I was in."

In this regard, the Mediterranean cultures may have something to teach us. It is still common to find an Italian widow wearing black clothes that clearly identify her as someone who is grieving. I've also seen stationery with a black border and, on occasion, men wearing black armbands. Each of these symbols reminds us that something significant has happened in the lives of those who use them.

If you, like Arlene, feel people aren't listening to your feelings, then consider adopting a symbol that will remind the people around you of your situation. Without a sign, those who don't know you simply won't understand that you are grieving.

Unfortunately, even if they can see and understand that you have recently lost someone very close to you, many people have difficulty giving you permission to grieve. It can be very uncomfortable for them to watch you cry or moan, or feel sad, or get angry, especially if they have never been exposed to death or grief before. Kathy summed it up:

"While Paul was dying, and then again after-wards, everyone told me what to do, what to think, and what to feel. No one said, go with the hurt. They all tried to talk me out of it."

As an analogy, imagine that you have a heart condition. It would seem ridiculous if you said to your friends or relatives, "Do you mind if I have a heart attack in front of you?" Unless they are skilled at treating the condition, the answer would likely be, "Are you kidding? I wouldn't know what to do. I wouldn't know how to handle it. That situation would be very frightening for me." In an ideal world, anyone about to have a heart attack would do so with a doctor present who could cope with what was going on.

Grief isn't much different. Just as no one wants to watch your heart stop, most people don't want you to grieve in front of them. They feel awkward and uncomfortable, and as a consequence will often say things that are not very helpful. They don't mean to be unsympathetic, but they simply don't know what to say. Although they have good intentions, they often create rather than solve problems. Kathy explains it like this:

> *"When something reminds me of Paul, and sadness overtakes me, it can be infuriating when people say things like, 'It will be okay' or 'Don't worry.' At those moments, I feel like it's the end of the world and things don't seem like they will ever be okay again."*

Her friends may be right. Her sadness may not be the end of the world, but, at that moment, the truth isn't nearly as important as the way Kathy feels.

> *"For the first while, I would build up anger and resentment toward my friends who patronized me, and then I had to deal with my anger, as well as my sadness. It all seemed overwhelming. Finally, I decided to confront the problem head-on. When people tried to talk me out of my feelings, I would let them know that I appreciated that they meant well. Then I would tell them just how real my pain was, and that I really needed them to simply stay close and support me. I was surprised just*

how well that worked. They accepted my direc-
tions and felt more comfortable dealing with me.
I didn't get so angry, and then I was able to deal
with my sadness more effectively."

That was Kathy's way of obtaining permission for herself to feel sad. It gave those near her permission to stay
close without feeling like they had to make things better.
"I don't want you to fix my sadness," she would say. "I
only want you near me."

Peter had a similar experience with his family and
friends. He finally developed a creative way of explain-
ing to people how hurt he felt:

"Years ago I broke my arm and had to have it in
a cast for several weeks. Everyone could see that
I was hurt and couldn't do certain things. I got
sympathy, attention, and understanding from
everyone because they knew that it would take
a long time for my broken arm to mend. Now I
have a broken heart. Even though you can't see
my broken heart, it will take much longer to heal
than my arm."

People received Peter's story well, hearing what he was
saying. It let everybody off the hook. By declaring loud
and clear that something about him hurt, he got permission to act accordingly. People around him did not

feel as awkward when he cried or lamented or looked lost.

When you are unwell, you probably visit your doctor, and often you may be prescribed pills to fix you up quickly. When you are grieving or sad, people tend to want you to get better as quickly as possible. I can't count the number of times I've heard someone say, "You need a sedative, a sleeping pill, or a tranquilizer to settle you down." What a perfect way to suggest to you that you're doing something wrong, that you're not acting appropriately. If you are grieving the loss of your partner or someone very close to you, you are bound to be upset. You have every reason to be upset. You need to be upset. Taking a sleeping pill only applies a mask, or a band-aid to the situation. It suppresses the feelings that need to happen. I've heard dozens of times, "Mother's not going to sleep tonight, she's so upset." Indeed, she has every reason to be upset, and does not need her grief stifled by a pill. Some things simply cannot be fixed quickly, especially with a pill. Of course, sometimes we may need medication to help us through, but pills are not necessarily the answer to every problem.

Although it's a crude one, food poisoning is a good analogy for grief. If you've eaten bad food, the sooner you vomit it up, the faster you'll recover. If you don't, the poisons could affect your whole system and make you very sick.

Your emotions, like toxic food, bubble around inside you and need to be released. Grief and the feelings that go along with it will not go away if you ignore them. You need to find ways to express your hurt. You need to give yourself permission to get rid of your awful feelings of anger, despair, and sadness. The sooner you let them out, the sooner you will begin to heal yourself and move on. Cry, scream, get angry, find someone who will listen and stay close to you. If you are not surrounded by obvious supporters, find a therapist, find a bereavement group, and find some avenue of expression. You are experiencing raw, new, frightening emotions that need to be exorcised. If you don't find some place that's safe to work through your emotions, you may well live with your grief for much longer than you ever imagined.

The Three Rs

Words like "stages" or "phases" tend to stereotype people's reactions to grief. Your feelings are yours alone, and they need to be dealt with individually. However, there are three reactions to the death of a loved one that you will sooner or later need to go through. My colleague the Reverend A. Tipping described these to me as "the three Rs," and I use them because I think they make practical sense.

The first R is *realize*:

Realize that the person has died, and realize the pain that that loss holds for you.

Realizing that someone has died sounds like it should be simple. But if you've just had someone you love die and you are overcome with sadness, some of the most basic things can become very confusing. Joan told me she spent weeks looking for her husband, Harold:

> *"I'd expect him at the door. I'd wait for a telephone call from him. I'd wake in the morning and expect him to be next to me in bed. I saw him die, but I couldn't take it in. It took me weeks to finally grasp what had happened."*

Peter had a similar reaction:

> *"For the first few days I visited places that I knew my wife would often go to. I hoped that somehow she was there, and not gone forever."*

These responses to loss are not as odd as they might sound. Once you've spent years developing patterns with someone, it can be very difficult to suddenly break those habits.

Retirement is like that. Your body develops several internal rhythms of its own. When you have spent years getting up at 6:30 in the morning to prepare for work, retirement will not immediately signal your body that there has been a change. It has been tuned to rising at a certain hour, and simply telling yourself that you no longer have to get up for work will make little difference. You must adjust and adapt to your new situation; in time, you will realize that you no longer need to be up so early.

Realizing that someone with whom you've had a long relationship has died takes time and work. More than likely, you will continue to look for the person for some time after he or she has died. Patrick would intentionally walk through crowded malls and streets, trying to find Jessie.

"It got so bad I began to wear sunglasses so that people couldn't see me. I wouldn't just glance, I'd stare into their faces, and you know, it sounds crazy, but I really expected to find her staring back at me. She couldn't be gone forever. Nothing is forever!"

Louise was even clearer about how hard it was for her to begin to realize Carl had died:

"I was constantly checking the mail, waiting for the phone to ring, and looking for a message on my answering machine telling me that Carl was holidaying in a faraway place because he just needed a holiday on his own. I even wondered if he'd run off with another woman and was frightened to tell me. Even that would have been okay. I would have forgiven anything to have him back."

To realize the pain that that loss holds for you is even more difficult. You must allow yourself to feel the effect of the loss of your loved one. In doing so you give yourself permission to feel deserted, lonely, sad, angry, lost, or whatever you need to feel after you first find out that your loved one has died. It's a bit like dental repair or minor surgery. As unpleasant as these experiences are to most of us, we feel very little after the local anaesthetic has been applied, and the numbness usually lasts for one or two hours after the work is completed. But when the freezing wears off, we begin to feel the pain, and we know that something significant has happened. That's the time when we start to look for some relief from the pain.

Beginning to realize the pain that the loss of your loved one holds for you is very similar. Now, after many days, or even weeks, you begin to know what has happened, and it hurts. Robert told me he was fine until he was left alone after the funeral:

> "I remember all those friends and relatives calling and coming to my home. So much food and non-stop action. It was almost like a party that went on and on. I was more like the host than someone in pain. I don't remember hurting much at all until it was all over and I was on my own."

Unfortunately, all of the fuss and attention do not last long, and soon the reality of the situation settles in.

Janice remembers that at the funeral she felt like she was watching a film:

> *"It was someone else's problem, not mine. It was unreal, like going to the movies. I thought that when the lights would come on, it would all have been some kind of crazy ride. But when everyone was gone, I knew that this was no show. It was real and so was the pain. I remember the first night. I held Morris's housecoat and simply cried into it."*

I have come to believe that the sooner you begin to realize the person has died, and how painful that death is for you, the sooner you will begin the hurtful – but necessary – grief process. Then, and only then, can you begin to have some sense of, and begin to work at the second R, as Linda discovered:

> *"I kept myself surrounded with friendly faces for days. I didn't have time to realize what had happened, or to feel the pain of my loss. Then, after a couple of weeks, when I was finally all alone, I felt awful. I was so lonely, so sad, so confused. If I could have avoided those feelings forever, I would have."*

The second R is *recognize*:

Recognize the significance of this loss for you and your life.

This can be an enormous task, especially if we are talking about the death of your partner. To do this you need to really understand how your life will be changed because your partner, your lover, your companion, your confidant has died. You need to recognize that the responsibilities you once shared are now yours, and yours alone. The habits that you developed together have to be altered. The plans and dreams you shared for the future are gone forever. Arthur described the impact of his wife's death on his life:

> "We travelled together. We did everything together. For nineteen years I could hardly wait to get home from work at night, home to her. I can never remember a time when she wasn't waiting, wasn't happy to see me. Now, I can't find a reason to go home at all. With her death I lost my right arm, and then some. Now I'm all on my own."

Frank, like Arthur, found the adjustment very difficult:

> "I remember what a wonderful Saturday-morning routine we had. For seven years we did the same thing with very few exceptions. I would get out of bed at about 8:00, get dressed, and almost run to

the store to get the newspaper. If I hurried, I could make that trip in about four minutes. While I was out, Claire would make the coffee, and I remember the smell that would greet me when I returned. We'd take the paper and coffee back to bed until about 10:00 so that we could enjoy it together. I loved Saturday mornings. Now, who cares? I haven't enjoyed the paper since she died."

For many people, gaining some understanding of the significance of the loss for their lives now and in the future will take a very long time. Usually all the days of the calendar must pass once so that we can experience each day for the first time without the one who has died. Heather and Valerie recalled the first few months:

"Every day was a new day without Doug. I had to face being alone, and all of the consequences that went with it. He wasn't there for my birthday, our anniversary, or Christmas. On the days I needed to see him most, I was simply on my own. I tried to cope. It took me months to recognize how my life had changed forever."

"You know, Ian's been dead for four months and I've only just begun to figure out that the Alaskan cruise that we were going to take next year has gone with him. I mentioned that to my friend and

she said, 'Take someone else.' Doesn't she know it's not the same? That trip without Ian means nothing to me."

When I was a child, my pet dog was killed by a car. My father was so upset and uncomfortable with my crying that he said, "Don't worry, we'll get you another puppy." My response was very fitting: "I don't want another puppy. I want *my* puppy." The grief of a child acknowledging that there is no substitute or replacement is profound. For you as an adult, there is no replacing your loved one either. You must take time to take stock of where you are, what's been taken from you, and what you've been left with. Then, and only then, can you move on eventually to the third R.

The third and final R is *rebuild*:

Rebuild your life without the person who has died.

Once you've really begun to understand the significance of your loss, and have begun to see what you're left with, then, and only then, can you move on to rebuild. In rebuilding, you find new ways to look at life, new activities to fill your days, and, for some, new relationships to meet your needs, *without* the person who has died. Bonnie kept telling me that all she wanted was her old life back:

"I don't want things to be new and different. I simply want Larry back. I simply want what was. It was good and I enjoyed it. I don't want any change."

It's very easy to understand exactly what Bonnie was talking about. Unfortunately, that is no longer possible for her.

With the death of your partner, the foundation of your life, your main relationship, is gone and you must learn to do things all over again. You may have to learn to socialize again, even though you may not have thought about meeting new people for a very long time. You may also have to give up many things you thought were safe and secure, like the habits you developed together that became second nature, but are now not so readily accepted by others.

Often, people try to rebuild early on in their grief. Robert was dating within six weeks of his wife's death:

"It hurts so much to think of her gone. In order to cope with my loss, I decided to try and ignore it. I guess I know I shouldn't be thinking about a relationship yet, but it makes me think that I can concentrate on something good and ignore the hurt."

Robert found that he couldn't cope. He kept thinking about his late wife, and his new relationships went nowhere. Rebuilding must not be rushed into. It wasn't until Robert truly realized that his wife had died, realized the pain that went along with her death, and recognized how his loss affected and altered his life, that he could think about rebuilding his life.

Often it seems that, if family and friends had their way, the griever would "get on with life" immediately. But until you have really taken the time and the energy to go through the first two Rs, rebuilding your life in a new and creative way will be impossible.

For some, rebuilding is very difficult. Alex was married for sixty-four years when his wife, Beverly, died. He was so lost. It was easy enough for him to realize the loss that had occurred, to realize the pain that came with her death, and to recognize the significance of her death. But rebuilding his life was another story. "I have made a conscious promise to myself," he would say. "I can never and will never fully enjoy life again. Without Beverly by my side, it's all a pale imitation." As long as Alex feels that way, it will be that way.

One of the keys to rebuilding your life without the person who has died is desire. Without the desire to go on, to improve things for yourself, things may never look much better to you, no matter how long it has been since your partner's death. As Valerie discovered, rebuilding her life was difficult but possible:

"It seemed to take forever. A sea of tears, a mountain of unrest, but you know I'm beginning to put

*it behind me, and finally, after months, I'm begin-
ning to think about getting on with my life."*

The Effects of Grief

Although grief can affect you in many different ways,
there are two specific places where grief will touch you:
your heart and your head.

At first, grief tends to touch our hearts. The next part
of this book focuses on the principal emotions that you
will have to struggle with as you deal with your grief:
loneliness, anger, guilt, and hopelessness. As you experience these emotions, they may not make any sense to
anyone but you. They will cause you to question your
existence, your reasons for going on, and may push you
to emotional depths that you have never experienced
before, as you struggle with your broken heart.

The last part of this book focuses on all of the other
things that grief will do to you as it affects your life. You
will experience changes in your outlook and perspective, alterations in your relationships with your family,
friends, and everyone you come into contact with. You
may question your beliefs and religious values as you re-
evaluate your life and your future. In the end, your grief
will leave you a very different person.

II

the heart

Recognizing Effects on Your Emotions

Loneliness

People experience many emotions or feelings during their grief. One of the most common is loneliness. It may result from a variety of different factors, and the intensity usually varies considerably from hour to hour, from day to day. You will probably find that it comes in waves. You may be feeling fine and then, suddenly, something will trigger the hurt and you'll be feeling raw all over again, just as though the one you're missing had died yesterday. You may feel the way Robert or Heather did:

"I am just so sad all the time, so incredibly lonely and empty. I walk down the street, wondering how

people can go on. Don't they know what has hap-
pened? Don't they know how terrible this is? Can't
people see the huge hole in me? Can't they see
how utterly lost I am?"

"Sometimes the loneliness is strongest in places
where there are lots of people: a grocery store, a
shopping mall. Everyone seems to be with some-
one. Everybody seems to have a goal or a purpose.
I just feel like my insides have been taken away
and I am an empty shell. At times the strangest
things will cause me to lose it: hearing laughter
or a baby crying, seeing people looking happy
together. No matter where I am, I have to stop
and cry. I must look like a fool. I've gotten used to
wearing sunglasses everywhere; it's less awkward
than having people staring because I am crying."

Yvette told me that the worst part of her grief is the
empty house and Gary's empty chair:

"Even though we didn't do everything together, he
was always there when I got home. Now, no matter
how well I fill my hours and my days, when I come
home the house is always quiet and lonely, and I
feel even more lonely when I see his empty chair.
I can be out having a terrific time and manage to
forget it all, but the minute I come home it starts

*all over again. There's no one to greet me, and no
one to sit and talk to."*

Douglas was feeling okay until he first sat at the
dining-room table. There was Chris's chair, empty. One
look at it and his loneliness became incapacitating, even
though he was with three of his close friends. It took several days, but he finally solved that problem by moving
to sit in her chair at the table, so that he wasn't staring at
the empty reminder all the time.

Cathy recalled the empty bed:

*"There's no one to hug, to kiss, to snuggle up to;
there's no one to hold on to, no one to be close to.
I've managed somehow to cope with the rest, but
I'm so tired of sleeping alone in our bed."*

I remember being called to a death in our emergency
room. After spending some time with a woman whose
husband had died suddenly of a heart attack, she turned
and said, "He promised he'd never leave me; he promised he'd always be there."

Even though death may not be a time to blame, we
often do. Couples make commitments to each other,
parents make promises to children, friends look forward
together, and when one of the people in the relationship
dies, the other often feels betrayed or abandoned. So
many of the things that you felt were certain, the things

you counted on, disappear forever when the one you love dies. After your friends and relatives have returned to their homes and their families, you are left alone.

Tracy told me:

"I wake every morning expecting Sam to be back in bed beside me. I pinch myself; hoping it's all been some kind of extended nightmare, hoping that finally he'll be where he belongs."

Laurie had a different experience:

"It's the strangest thing. It's as though James had never existed. We were married more than forty years and knew some of our friends for almost as long. But now, many of them, particularly our good friends, never mention his name. After all the times we shared together, it makes me angry. They weren't just my friends, they were our friends. I guess they just don't know what to say."

When your partner dies, you may lose some of the friends you thought were there for life. People become awkward around you and too uncomfortable to talk about your partner. They don't know how to approach the subject. Many decide it's better never to say anything for fear you might become upset. Indeed, you probably would be saddened by such a conversation, but what's wrong with that? Losing your partner is very upsetting.

Patrick describes this as feeling like a "fifth wheel."

"When Jessie was alive, we had so many friends and went to so many activities together. Now I'm lucky if I get an invitation at all, and if I go, I feel like a 'fifth wheel.' Everybody else is usually in pairs, and they often seem uncomfortable with my presence. So, most of the time I simply stay at home. It's just not worth it."

Frank tells of his similar experience:

"You'd think I had some kind of awful disease. People treat me like I have leprosy. I go to places that I've been going to for ages, and I can feel how awkward people are. Many don't know what to say to me, so they avoid me altogether and say nothing at all. Maybe I am overly sensitive, but people just don't know what to do with me. It makes me feel like I've done something wrong, that this lonely situation I'm in is somehow my own fault."

"Widow" and "widower" are strange labels. You are no longer married, even though you may still wear a wedding band, and even though you may be very much alone, you don't feel single. After working with Bernie for many months, I recall asking why he still wore his wedding ring. "Well, I'm married," he snapped. Then he thought for a moment and said, "I'm not, am I? I'm really not. But I still feel so married."

Friends may avoid contacting someone whose partner has died, as Marilyn discovered:

> *"Nobody telephones. 'We'll call you. We'll get together.' That's what they all say. But they rarely do, and when they do call, it feels strained or phony."*

Laura told me she doesn't get many calls now because she figures she's a threat to other women:

> *"You'd think I was going to steal their husbands. I can't believe it. Now I'm treated like an eligible, single woman instead of an old friend."*

Most of us are familiar with Charles Dickens's masterpiece A *Christmas Carol*. Poor old Ebenezer Scrooge has a dreadful Christmas Eve. He's visited by three ghosts. Of those ghosts, the one most frightening to Scrooge is the ghost of Christmas yet to come, the ghost that shows him what things will be like. If you're grieving the loss of a partner, then to many you are a reminder of what they may have to face one day. Since people don't like to think unpleasant thoughts, you, like Patrick or Frank, may be left alone, or at least made to feel awkward.

The loneliness will pass eventually, but only if you spend a great deal of time working with your feelings. Feel sad when you're sad. Feel angry when you're angry. Cry if you need to. Tell someone how alone you are, how lonely you feel, and with time those feelings will finally become manageable. You'll always remember them, but they won't be foremost in your mind all the time.

Some people try to cope with the loneliness by getting a pet. It provides them with something to love and care for. A pet can be a terrific idea. It can fill many gaps. It can be warm and responsive, but is no substitute for the person who has died.

Valerie was amazed at her own progress. After almost two years, she told me:

> *"I don't cry all the time, and most of the time I don't even feel like crying. I'm aware that Anthony's gone and that's awful. But now I can get on with my life and it only hurts a little at a time. I can hardly believe it!"*

Anger

When people who are grieving talk about losing someone very close to them, they most often liken it to feeling as if they've had something that they didn't want to let go of ripped or torn from them. They feel helpless and powerless as they watch their partner slip away from them. Then they feel anger and rage at their helplessness, their powerlessness, and their loss.

Marcel doesn't know who he's angry at: God, the medical staff, or even his wife for dying and leaving him alone. But, he knows that sometimes the loneliness is so acute, and the feeling of unfairness so powerful, that he can hardly stand it.

Anger is a feeling that can consume you when you're grieving. It can be triggered by many different things. The rest of the world seems to be doing fine. No one else is crying or grieving, and no one understands. That can make you even angrier.

Usually, when significant changes occur in our lives, we choose to make them. We choose our jobs, our spouses, our homes, and usually we choose if and when to have children. But death chooses us. We have no say in the matter, unless we choose suicide.

Tina told me she's angry at the drastic change in her life. She just wants things to be the way they were:

> "I didn't have any say in this, no choice at all. My life was fine, great in fact. My husband, William, and I worked hard all our lives and, just when we were getting ready to retire, William got sick and died before we had a chance to enjoy things."

Anger at Being Left Alone

Loneliness can cause anger and resentment. Maggie told me how she felt:

> "When I realize that Don has died and gone forever, I get so angry thinking that I'm left with a ruined life. Sometimes I just want to throw

*something. Often I'll go into the bedroom and
pound my fists on the bed. I know it won't bring
him back, but it makes me feel better."*

Laurie recalls the anger she felt after Mark died:

*"My jobs and his jobs, they're all mine now. We
agreed to take on our responsibilities as a team, and
now I'm the only player. He left it all in my hands. I
don't know how to fix things. I don't even know how
to service the car. It's not right. It's not fair."*

Ruth told me she feels guilty saying it, but after David
died she felt angry every time she saw an elderly person:

*"They've lived their life. They've had their chance,
and yet they're alive and my husband died so
young. In some cases these people are almost
twice his age. It's just not fair."*

You may become angry with those close to you.
Friends and family members usually want to help, but
often end up putting their foot in their mouth. It's very
easy to feel patronized by them. Even though they have
good intentions, their clichés can make you very angry:

"Be thankful for all the good times you had together."
"His suffering is over now."

"She's gone to a better place."
"There will be another special person for you."
"It was God's will."

Well-meaning statements like these can cause you to boil. It's often a very fine line between saying nothing and blowing up at people when you hear things that make you angry. My advice is to be honest. Acknowledge that you know they are trying to help, but that what they've said causes you pain. By doing so you will let those close to you know how you feel, and be able to release your feelings without necessarily offending anyone.

Penny knew Jack had cancer and that his disease was very serious. But, after Jack died, Penny became consumed with anger toward his physician:

"He was doing so well. I thought he was better, then he up and died. His doctor must have done something wrong."

The right or wrong seems insignificant now that Jack is dead. What matters is that Penny has been left full of anger at the unfair twist of life. She needed to have somewhere to direct it, and Jack's doctor became the target of her anger. For over a year Penny was unable to get on with her grief and her life because she was so full of rage.

Storing up anger inside of you isn't a good idea. Without warning, you may find yourself snapping at people who are close to you, or challenging people who you aren't angry with.

Brenda finds herself picking fights with people in grocery stores who stand in the wrong line or who butt in. She would have never done that in the past.

"I get fed up quickly and easily, and don't like being pushed around. After Henry died, I got even touchier."

Fred is a man of forty-one whose wife died almost a year ago after a three-year battle with breast cancer. He finds himself filled with anger at people whom he calls fixers:

"I'm so tired of people trying to make everything better.

"I've had so much advice, so much information about what would help, what would make me feel better: Take a vacation. Get a new job. Go back to work soon. Try to forget the past. Start dating; you're younger than you think. Look to the future. Put the past behind you. These people, these fixers, make me so angry. I know they all mean well, but I am so tired of well-meaning people who have all the answers for my life.

*"I was so vulnerable, I found myself doing what
I was told. I took a trip, it didn't help. I went back
to work too soon, and I couldn't function properly.
I even tried dating, and I ended up feeling like a
fool because I wasn't ready.*

*"I know the buck stops with me. I am an adult,
and I have to take responsibility for my actions. If
only people had let me hurt, let me grieve, let me
be a mess until I didn't need to be a mess anymore."*

Fred's anger at the fixers in his life is easy to understand.
Not only does he have to cope with his grief, but he must
also deal with his anger and resentment toward those
who were too uncomfortable to let him hurt and ended
up stifling his feelings. These days Fred and I have been
trying to cope with his anger with himself for being so
susceptible to everyone else's point of view. How easily
that can happen when you are feeling alone and needy.

Margo had a similar experience with others who
thought they knew what was best for her:

*"I swear, the whole world wanted me to start another
relationship right away. Friends and family had all
these eligible men for me to meet. Thank goodness I
didn't pay attention. Sure I'm far too young to be a
widow, but I felt so angry, so cheated when people
tried to rush me into another relationship just so
they wouldn't have to worry about me anymore."*

Walter gets furious when people say they understand his grief:

> *"I feel so cheated, so patronized, so hurt by their cheap words. How can they possibly understand? Their spouse is still alive. Nothing turns me off more than when people tell me they understand. They haven't been where I've been. They haven't experienced the loss that I've had."*

Instead of being honest and saying that they can't imagine how you feel, or how much you hurt, many people feel they need to pretend that they do understand. As Walter said, "I feel so angry, so sick, so patronized with their cheap words. I wish they would just stop and listen to me."

If you are filled with rage over the unfairness of death, I encourage you to find a way to let it out. Find someone to talk to about just how upset you are; someone who can hear your anger without judgment; someone who will stay with you no matter how angry you get.

I also suggest exercising to get rid of your frustrations. Tennis, squash, and racquetball are particularly good as they allow you to make contact with something, rather than someone. Even a punching bag may not be a bad idea. Making contact with something won't solve your anger, but it will give you another outlet for expressing yourself.

Kevin writes letters to the government when he gets upset:

"Since my wife died, I get irritated much more easily than before. I find that simply putting my anger onto paper makes it all seem easier."

After Joe died, I encouraged Sandra to write a letter to Joe's doctor, expressing her anger. It took her a long time to do it, but after she wrote her anger down, she felt much better. Finally she decided not to send the letter as she had found relief simply by writing her thoughts down. You may find it more useful to communicate your anger constructively to the person responsible for it. Only you can decide what's best for you.

Nothing could be more frustrating than having someone you love die. You want things to be the way they were. When they're not, you can get very angry. In time the anger and pain will fade. But, things will never be the same again.

It's a lot like surgery. Initially, the wound is red and sore. Slowly the soreness passes. The wound turns purple, then pink, and finally fades to a white scar. But even if you live a hundred years, the scar will still be there. Your body will never look the same again.

However you do it, I encourage you to express your anger and pain. Until you can get rid of your rage, it will haunt you.

Guilt

Guilt is one of those feelings that either we possess in abundance or we do not. If we do feel guilt, it can be a terrible emotion to deal with, and one that is not easily conquered. For many it begins during a partner's illness, as it did for Peter:

"Beth had always been the strong, healthy one in our relationship. I had been very ill twice in our marriage and she had nursed me back to health. She was one of those people who had never really been sick a day in her life. If she wasn't feeling well, she would say little, if anything at all. As for me, I needed a lot of comforting, even if I only got a cold.

*Then, when she got cancer, I couldn't believe it.
They told me she had a brain tumour. I was para-
lyzed by my horror. It should have been me. It just
wasn't right. I would go home at night and pray
that we could change places. It must have been
some kind of mistake! She had cared for me, and
now when it was my turn to look after her, there
wasn't a thing that I could do. I felt so guilty."*

Peter's feelings are not uncommon. So often the helplessness that you feel standing beside your loved one's
bed can turn into guilt that you're okay and he or she is
not. That can be a terrible burden to carry around.

For many, after a partner dies, the guilt continues, or
even gets worse. Michelle described it this way:

*"Sometimes I go out and have a bit of fun. Then out
of the blue it hits me. How can I, how dare I, have
fun when Wayne is dead? He can't enjoy himself.
We can't enjoy things together, so I shouldn't be
having any fun either. It's nuts! Sometimes when
I'm in the middle of a smile or a laugh, I think of
Wayne and I start to cry. I think I feel guilty every
time I take a breath and enjoy it."*

Like Michelle, if you've been used to doing fun or enjoy-
able things with the person you've lost, it can often feel
wrong to do those same things on your own.

Guilt can also arise from many questions for which we simply don't have reasonable answers, as Walter discovered:

> *"Sometimes I have strange thoughts. I'm no saint and at times in our relationship I have made mistakes. Now I often think my wife got sick and died because I did things wrong. I try to force those thoughts out of my mind, but they tear me apart. If I thought that I was somehow responsible for what happened to her, I would go crazy."*

If you can remember that our feelings are often not based on things that make sense as we understand them, then that may be of some help. Guilt over your loved one's death is a very real feeling and you need to accept it as such, but you do not have to accept it as reasonable or true. Our emotions are often not based in truth, only in feeling.

Margaret is almost ninety. Lucas, to whom she was married for nearly seventy years, died over a year ago from pneumonia after a long stay in hospital. Margaret feels responsible for his death, because one day, after a rainstorm, she suggested that they walk to the corner store to buy a newspaper. As they made that short journey, Lucas slipped on a wet spot on the pavement and broke his hip. He survived the surgery very well, but, unfortunately, near the end of his stay in hospital he developed pneumonia and died.

"I killed him, you know. If I hadn't wanted a newspaper so badly, Lucas would still be alive today. It's like I took a gun and shot him myself."

Margaret's guilt is very real and very painful. Even though she knows that Lucas was simply a victim of circumstance, she needs to feel her guilt and speak of it.

Guilt is expressed in many different forms. Richard has attempted to get close to other women since his wife, Cynthia, died, at age thirty-five. Although it's been more than two years since she died, he still feels like he is letting Cynthia down each time he gets close to another woman:

"How can I go out with other women? How can I have romantic intentions when Cynthia's memory is so strong? Every time I get close to someone else, I see the strangest things. I remember the first time I met Cynthia. I remember the night we became engaged. I remember our wedding day and our wedding night. I know I took a vow that I would be faithful to her alone until death do us part, but these images are still haunting me. I feel like I'm betraying her trust being with other women."

It's very important to remember to do things when you are ready, not when others are ready for you to do them. When Richard is ready to begin to see other women, he will let himself off the guilty hook that he is on. If people do things before they are ready, then their needs won't be met.

Guilt can also come from trying to live up to the expectations of others. So many times I've heard people say, "My friends/family/co-workers expect me to be in a different space than where I actually am. That makes me feel guilty, angry, and like a failure." Eugene and Roy express their anger at others' expectations of them:

> "If I hear another person say, 'Well, it's been a year, it's time for you to be getting on with your life,' I'll go mad! How do they know when it's time for me to get on with my life?"

> "Everyone has expectations for me. I wonder how many of these people who are so keen to be an expert have worn my shoes. What do they know? It's my life anyway."

The combination of guilt and anger will rise quickly if you're surrounded by people who are sure that they know what's best for you. When people try to tell you where you ought to be, a simple "I'm not ready yet," or "I'm still too shaky," or "I hope that will come one day" will tell people that you are not yet ready.

It is helpful to speak about guilt without being judged or talked into or out of it. In time, if you receive permission to feel your guilt, and give yourself permission to let it go, you will move beyond it, or at least put it into a manageable perspective.

Hopelessness

Having someone you love die brings you face to face with some very difficult and painful emotions. One of the most difficult to get through is the feeling of hopelessness.

After the person has died, you are brought face to face with a terrible struggle. Does death take away all hope? Has it all been for nothing? Is there any point to anything at all?

For a time, all of the hope you had for the person now gone, and for yourself, may well vanish. There seems to be little reason to carry on. All of the things you dreamt of seem to be in ruins.

Bob described it like this:

"It was like I'd fallen into a pit with very slippery sides. Nothing in it, and when I thought about getting out of it, I couldn't scale the sides anyway. It all seemed utterly hopeless. Things I'd spent years looking forward to and hoping for, all died with her. Shrugging my shoulders at the thought of the future was the best I could do."

I have likened the death of a partner, or of anyone very close to you, to the experience of being in a tent when someone unexpectedly takes away the centre pole. In an instant there is darkness, shock, confusion, and a terrible feeling of being lost. In fact, that feeling of being lost and empty can cause you physical pain – in your stomach or your head – that can be far worse than a broken bone or a cut, and remind you regularly that you're alone, that you've got no place to go.

John had a friend whose wife died two years ago:

"It was a terrible time for Roman. I'd sit with him. Try to comfort him. Take him out to dinner. Just be a friend. I soon got used to watching him cry. That took some doing as his tears really made me uncomfortable. Some of the things he would tell me didn't make any sense to me. He would talk of emptiness, of feeling lost, of feeling hopeless.

"These days I understand what he meant. Two months ago my wife was killed in a car accident. Now I've got this aching pain in my head and stomach that reminds me of what Roman was talking about. It's a strange thing to say but I feel like an orphan because there is no one who can care for me the way she did."

Barbara explained how hopeless she felt:

"I feel so empty. A huge part of me has been blown away. I wake in the morning and, for a split second, I have forgotten; and then the pain all floods back and I feel so empty, like a shell that has had the oyster taken out of it. It feels like there is no future, no reason to go on, no reason to be happy."

Barbara's and John's feelings are not unusual. The realization of what has happened, and the recognition of what it all means, can cause terrible despair.

Bernie felt that there simply wasn't a happy ending for him:

"I've been going through life believing in happy endings as though I lived in a fantasy. I always thought that Elizabeth and I were going to be okay. We'd been through so much together. Hard times, even times when there was no money, but

we always had each other, and we believed that
we were going to live happily ever after. Now that
hope for a tomorrow, for happiness, for a good
ending, is really gone. I feel so lost, so empty."

For those around you, your feelings of hopelessness will be some of the most difficult emotions that they will have to deal with. They may feel a need to convince you that you're going to be okay. That there is a tomorrow. That you still have a future. But none of these things will make much sense to you when your loved one dies.

This sense of hopelessness has also been described to me as futility and despair, as something heavy that weighs you down. Debbie told me she feels much older, much slower:

"I used to be able to get lots accomplished in a
day. Now it all seems pointless. I don't seem to
care about anything, and it takes all of my energy
to just keep myself going. Previously, I had always
hated the rain. It was wet, and spoiled a nice day.
Now I look forward to it. The water falling out of
the sky, the darkness, and the thunder, all seem
to fit in perfectly with my mood. You're going
to think I'm crazy, but at least it feels like the
weather understands. Last week it rained twice,
and each time I went and sat on a bench in the
middle of it."

It didn't sound crazy to me. It sounded like Debbie was feeling so lost and empty that she needed something symbolic that would touch her hopelessness, something that would express just what she was feeling. There are no words to take away this feeling of hopelessness. I'm not sure it can be understood by anyone who has not been there, but it can be expressed to anyone who will listen, and in time, it will pass.

In time, you will once again hope and dream. You might cling to a religious belief that gives you hope for the one who has died. You might simply mend in time and begin to see a future again. Peter told me that two things seemed to happen almost simultaneously:

"My sense of hopelessness and my fidgetiness seemed to go together. I'd get to the mall and feel like I needed to be home. I'd get home and feel like I needed to be out. It used to drive me crazy. Nothing made sense. I couldn't sit still. I couldn't care less, and I couldn't see a future. Now, after pacing for what seems like forever, looking face to face into bleakness for so long, I can see me down the road. It's amazing. I'm saying the same old cliché I used when my wife was sick – 'You've got to have something to hope for.' Now I'm hoping for me!"

III

the head

Recognizing Effects on Your Life

What's the Change?

There is no way to prepare for the unexpected death of someone you love. You can't rehearse it. It simply happens. The person is here one minute and gone the next. All death, even the ones that "we see coming," are unexpected.

Death is one of the most forbidden topics in our society. Most of us have never entered into a "what if" conversation about death, so when it comes suddenly, we are often left in shock with an unbelievably painful reality. As one woman, whose young husband was killed suddenly, said:

"This isn't real, is it? We have children, commitments, and a future planned together. This just can't be real. I know he'll be there when I go home."

She really knew better, but her words echoed so typically the disbelief we see when people face sudden death. Even with expected death things aren't much better. As Cathy and Douglas put it:

"Even though he was dying and we all knew it, even though he only lay there, not being able to communicate, he was still there."

"I cared for Chris for the last seven weeks of her life. I knew she would die, but, when it finally happened, I couldn't accept the fact that she was gone forever. I hoped that it was only a dream."

For many, as for Gail, with this shock, disbelief, and utter sadness come totally unexpected feelings that can cause us considerable confusion:

"What's happening to me? I coped so well through my husband's illness. I was strong; I was in control; I kept it all together under very difficult circumstances. Now I'm lost. I feel like I'm falling to pieces – worse than that, I feel like I'm going crazy."

While there are no certainties about our grief reactions, some are common and may very well happen to you. If you experience any or all of them, you're not going crazy, you're not exhibiting unusual behaviour, you're simply reacting to the trauma you've experienced as a result of the loss of your loved one. As with every reaction to grief, you must recognize the change and work through it. A few of the common grief reactions are discussed below.

Common Grief Reactions

Sleep Disturbance

As you grieve, your sleeping habits may change considerably. Some grievers "sleep all the time." Peter told me that sleep was his only ally, so he slept as often as possible and for many hours at a time.

Or, you may hardly be able to sleep at all. Rosa remembers:

> *"For the first six months I'd toss and turn for an hour or more before I could get to sleep. Then I'd only sleep for an hour or so before I'd wake up again. I spent hundreds of sleepless hours staring at the walls and ceiling."*

Others find they can get to sleep, but they wake much earlier in the morning than they're used to. Any change in sleep patterns can be very disturbing, especially if you're feeling tired and rundown. Although it's a temptation, consider well before you ask your physician for sleeping tablets. You can easily get used to them, and ultimately they only mask what's happening to you. You're not sleeping for a reason. You're lost. You hurt, and your life has been completely rearranged. When you can't sleep, consider calling a friend, reading a book, or watching TV. You might even write your feelings down, and on occasion cry yourself to sleep, as Linda did:

> *"I hate not sleeping. Sometimes if I can cry and get rid of my hurt, then I'm not so sad afterwards, and usually I fall asleep."*

Whatever you choose to do, it's better to work through your feelings than to cover up your grief.

Change in Appetite

Another reaction that often accompanies grief is a change in appetite. Kathy remembered what happened to her:

> *"I couldn't see the point to eating. I'd go a whole day and forget to eat. I really had no use for food. Only when I was grieving could I lose any weight, and I lost fifteen pounds before I started to feel better."*

Eating is a social activity. While we're grieving we're usually not feeling very social, and it is common for our food intake to decrease. A little weight loss is to be expected. But if you continue to lose weight, that can become unhealthy, and you should seek some assistance from your physician.

Albert was very creative in dealing with this problem. He knew he wasn't eating properly because he was so alone. So, a few months after his wife died, he rented a room in his home to a university student, just so he could have someone else to eat with. Albert found that the social interaction of eating quickly returned, and soon he was again enjoying his meals and eating well.

Lack of Motivation

Many grievers, like Valerie, experience a profound lack of mental or physical motivation, or both:

> *"I couldn't care less about getting up, getting dressed, getting going. I had no interest in anything for weeks."*

Lynn actually lost some of her ability to move. Not long after her husband, Malcolm, died, she found that she could hardly walk. For several weeks she had to use two canes to get around. While this was an extreme response to grief, it was very real and had to be dealt with seriously.

Things improved for both Valerie and Lynn when they found a chance to express their concerns, their sadness, and their feelings of uselessness. By simply talking to others about their pain, and how their systems were reacting to it, they both improved dramatically.

Some Grief Reactions That May Be Cause for Concern

Not all grief reactions are healthy. There are many reactions that may be unhealthy when taken in their context. The list is far too long to consider all of them here. If, in your grief, you are doing things very differently from the way you were doing them before, then you should seek assistance from someone who knows how to manage grief reactions. If you continue in isolation, your grief may go on much longer than you ever imagined, and it may impair your ability to rebuild your life.

Overworking

Many people find it easier to get right back to work than to spend several days absorbing what has happened to their lives and how significant their losses have really been. While this matter may be out of many grievers' control as most employers only permit two or three days off for bereavement leave, others prefer to immerse themselves in extra work so they won't have to deal with their grief.

If you are working to avoid your pain and your reality, you need to consider seriously the implications of your excessive activities. There is no doubt that grieving is work. It takes a long time and a lot of effort, and you won't be able to get on with your grieving if you're busy with everything else. Find someone who knows something about grief and share your feelings and your changed work habits with them. While it may be very painful to face your reality, discussing it with someone who understands will help you through it.

Increased Alcohol Intake

After the loss of someone they love, some people begin drinking excessively. Be careful of that. If your alcohol consumption has increased since your partner's death, you may have a problem.

Wilson drank only moderately and socially before his wife died. But after she died, alcohol was somehow much more acceptable to him than drugs as an escape:

"The pain would get so strong in the evenings that I would begin to drink. For the first couple of weeks it was three or four ounces of Scotch a night. It just soothed me, and let me sleep. Then after a few weeks I needed much more − seven, eight, or even ten ounces over two or three hours.

*It was nearly a year before I was prepared to admit
to myself and to my family that I had a problem."*

Drinking is just like taking a pill. It appears to be an instant fix for our feelings, while actually it only covers them up temporarily. Drinking may not seem to be a big deal to you now, but it may become a very big problem in your life if you let it continue. Don't be afraid to discuss this subject with someone you can trust, as soon as you realize that there is a change in your drinking habits. It's much easier to work through the grief that is driving the drinking before the drinking becomes a big problem itself.

Unnatural Attachment to Objects

Sometimes grief leads you to form an unnatural attachment to objects that belonged to the person who has died. You might be wearing an article of his clothing, or taking something of hers to bed with you. You might be refusing to let anyone sit in the dead person's favourite chair. You might resist packing up his clothing, or even rearranging his room. Whatever the case, if you have changed your attachment to something, discuss the change with someone. If it's all wrapped up in your grieving, you need assistance in sorting it out, or your grieving will continue for longer than necessary.

I want you to know, however, that some holding on to things is not necessarily cause for concern. Sleeping

in an old shirt of the person who has died or not want-
ing to get rid of their personal belongings until you feel
comfortable to do so is understandable.

You will know when you no longer need to hold on
in these ways.

Thoughts of Suicide

When we lose someone we love dearly, we sometimes
think of suicide. For even a few moments, many of us
may want to be with the person who has died, because
life seems to have lost all of its meaning. While our feelings of loneliness, emptiness, lack of motivation, and
pain may continue for some time, our thoughts of suicide usually subside quickly. However, if you continue
to consider suicide, or you have worked out a plan, you
need to share your thoughts with someone you can trust.
While it may not seem to be the case for you today, vir-
tually everyone I've ever worked with eventually finds
some life and light at the end of the long journey
through grief.

Whatever you're feeling, if it represents a big change in
your life, share it with someone who knows something
about grief. Don't continue to live in isolation.

Grief hurts a great deal. Because the pain is so intense,
and your life has been changed so dramatically, you will
almost certainly experience changes. Some are very pre-
dictable, so take heart that you have not gone crazy.

Other changes are not so expected. Be aware of them and, if they persist, discuss them with your doctor or a professional who knows how to handle grief.

Remember, only you can do the work that grief demands, but you don't have to do it alone.

Family and Friends

Family and friends can be very supportive or they may be of no help to you at all. Some people, like Michael, find family and friends to be supportive, positive, and even helpful:

"What would I have done without my children? Andrew is just twelve, and Joan fifteen. They've been so helpful. Even though they have their own grief and their own needs, they are so sensitive to my needs. When I get home from work I don't even have to open my mouth, and they know exactly what's going on with me. Often we'll sit and talk about Ellen, about things we did together, about

how we miss her. They're terrific! I never thought I'd be able to weep with my children. Although I've been very proud, we often cry over missing their mother."

Josephine had a similar experience with her friends:

"I've had these two close female friends for many years. It was only after Bud died that I began to know just how close we were. When everyone went their separate ways after the funeral, my friends stayed close. It's the tangible, physical things that I've been so grateful for. At dinnertime, when I had no energy to cook and little interest in eating, there was usually a knock on the door, and one of them was standing there with a home-made dinner for two. When they did their shopping, they would do mine too. When I was feeling down, one or both of them would come and sit with me, sometimes to cheer me up, sometimes just to be close. I had no idea that they cared for me so much."

The relationship you have with your family and friends after the death of your partner depends on two things. First, the role that your partner had within the family is very important. If your partner was the focal point of the family and friends, then the loss may split your family

and friends apart. Mary was the hub of Larry's family and
social activities:

> *"She was like a mother hen. The family was always
> huddled around her. She made all of the plans.
> She was the person everyone counted on to or-
> ganize birthdays, anniversaries, and Christmas
> gatherings. Now that she's gone, no one orga-
> nizes anything. We all act like strangers. No one
> feels comfortable filling her shoes, so now noth-
> ing happens."*

Mary's death left such a huge hole in Larry's family and
social life that now people are scattered. She had such a
key role that everyone else is lost without her direction.
Unfortunately, that leaves Larry on his own, feeling like
no one cares:

> *"She was so good at organizing. Now that she's
> gone, no one can be bothered doing anything. It
> makes me wonder if anyone remembers that I'm
> here all alone."*

In contrast, Natasha found that her family rallied to
fill the gap that was left when Jed died:

> *"My three daughters all try so hard to act as if
> their father isn't missing. They do all of the things*

that Jed did. It would have been our thirty-fifth wedding anniversary last week. They knew Jed would have made a big deal over it, so they took me out to dinner in his place. It was very sweet of them, but it wasn't the same."

Second, your relationship with family and friends will depend on the way that they interacted together previously. People tend to be consistent in character and habit. If your family was strong, close, caring, and supportive, then there is a good chance that that bond will continue. But if they were fragmented or not strongly supportive, then that will be unlikely to change. Rina told me that her family was always fragmented, with everyone off in her own direction, doing her own thing:

"I guess I've been kidding myself, but I thought that if anything was going to bring my family together, it would be Don's death. What a joke! My son never had much time for anyone but himself. Now he makes this huge effort and phones me every ten days or so, but he doesn't even mention his father! Recently my daughter sent me a Mother's Day card. Beyond that, she can't even be bothered to call. I should have expected it. That's exactly how things were before their father died. They'd call or write once in a while, but nothing more. I guess they're just being consistent."

Indeed, they are being consistent. Just as Josephine's friends and Michael's family were acting in a way that was in keeping with their past, so too did Rina's. Occasionally, people do change. They do more than you expect of them. But most people will be consistent, following patterns that have long been established. Remember, most people find change very difficult.

Families often find it hard to give permission to grieve to the person who has lost a partner. Again, there are two reasons for this. Although you have lost your partner, and suffered the biggest wound, you are not the only person who is grieving. Depending on their relationship with the person who has died, the people around you may be hurting so much that reaching out to you may be too painful. Morris described what happened in his family:

"We used to be so close to Connie's sisters and their husbands. Now they are so distant. When we do get together, they break down and cry whenever I mention Connie's name, and they often get up and leave the room. I feel like I should be helping them. They're certainly not able to do much for me."

Children may react in the same way. When Tanya's husband, Ralph, died, she thought her grown children would help her grieve, but they didn't:

"They never mention their father. They help in other ways, but if his name comes up, or something reminds them of him, they get so upset that it's simply not worth it."

In both cases, Morris's and Tanya's family members were so hurt, so full of their own pain, that they could do little, if anything, to help the person who had lost a partner. Even if they can overcome their own hurt, family and friends may find it very difficult to watch you cry and to see you lost, lonely, empty, and angry in your grief. A few months ago, a close friend of mine died. At times it was very difficult for me to care for his grieving family, as they were too close to me. To watch them cry was often more than I could bear, and at times I found it difficult not to turn away.

Paul described the problem better than anyone I know:

"My friends would get so uncomfortable with my pain and my tears that they would do anything to avoid them. When I would become sad, they'd practically stand on their heads to deflect my sadness or change my thoughts."

To watch a stranger grieve is painful. To watch someone you love or care for grieve may at times be too difficult to take. Families and friends can be a great strength and help to you as you grieve, especially if they've been able to help you in the past. But if that hasn't been your past experience, beware. They may also have many strong feelings about you and the person who has died, and it may be too difficult for them to reach out to you while you are grieving.

To help you through your grief, it can be very useful to negotiate with close family members and friends. Tell them what you feel you need from them. Allow them to respond honestly and tell you whether they can manage your request or not. It will give them fair warning about your expectations, and also help you understand their feelings and position.

Dates Can Be Painful
Reminders of a Loss

Grief is the process of working through your feelings after someone close to you has died. You are looking to rebuild your life in a new and positive way. The raw pain of grief can last a few months or several years, and during that time, particularly during the first year, you will have many new experiences that will be very difficult and painful.

Each Year Brings Many Special Dates

During the course of a year, there are many events and dates that we remember for special reasons. Some, like Christmas, New Year's Day, Easter, Mother's Day,

Father's Day, and Thanksgiving, are celebrated by almost everyone (your special holidays may be different, depending on your traditions). Others, like birthdays and anniversaries, are very personal events that have special meaning to us as individuals.

For many who lose those close to them, certain events like Christmas can trigger loneliness. Traditionally a special family time, a time to be with the ones we love, Christmas is often the only time in the year when the whole family gets together.

Marilyn recalled her first Christmas without Don. She stayed with her daughter, her son-in-law, and her granddaughter.

"Those few days couldn't pass quickly enough. All I could think of were the Christmases past when I would look forward to being with my husband, Don; to exchanging gifts; and to the excitement of the season. This year, I knew how excited the rest of my family was, but I felt so alone, and I just stayed in bed and cried."

January 15 has a special meaning for Laura. It was the first time she and her husband dated, and exactly a year later he proposed to her. Darlene remembers August 6 as the happiest day of her life. It was her wedding day, and for thirty-two years it was a sacred date that she and Jeremy spent together, alone.

When Someone Dies, Many Dates Take On New Meaning

When someone you love dies, new dates appear in your calendar, and old events take on new meanings. The date your loved one's illness was discovered, the date you learned that there wouldn't be any more treatment, the date he or she died – all loom as ugly memories that won't disappear.

Kevin remembers May 19 vividly. It was the day his wife died, quite unexpectedly. Since then, for a few days around the nineteenth of every month, he becomes sad and withdrawn, and some months he has even been physically ill.

Many people tell me that the first year after a death is the worst. It's the first time you experience each day alone – your first Christmas, your first birthday, and your first wedding anniversary without your partner. They all remind you that things will never be the same again. But the second year can be just as bad, or worse. Samantha told me that for her, the second year was more difficult than the first:

"I just couldn't take anything in during the first year. People were so surprised that I hurt more the second time around, but it was as if the first year had been a bad dream and I was just waking up. By the time my birthday came around for

the second time, I finally realized that Bill would
never be back, and then the pain really set in."

It isn't just the special dates of the year that are problems. A particular time of the day, or a day of the week,
can often be more difficult than any other time. Danny
tells me that the nights are so lonely:

"I can keep myself occupied during the day, but
it's so quiet, so lonely at night."

Andy tells me that Sundays are his worst days. They seem
to take forever. He and his wife had always tried to spend
them together, and now they are so empty.

Our Tendency Is to Run Away from the Pain

Part of grieving is to realize that these dates, or times of
the day, are difficult. The tendency for many is to run
from the pain they bring.

Douglas was a successful businessman when his wife,
Andrea, died of leukemia. He went immediately from
working forty to fifty hours a week to working eighty to
ninety hours a week. He kept himself so busy that he
didn't have time to think about anything but his work,
even on his "special dates."

As much as it's not a bad idea to keep busy, it's not a good idea to run away from the pain. There is much to be said for acknowledging how much it hurts to be alone and to recognize what special dates and times do to you. By understanding these feelings, these dates and times will become much more manageable as you rebuild your life. They may even become days when you once again celebrate the happy memories of the one you loved so much.

God, Where Were You When I Needed You Most?

Annie told me that she used to believe in God. She went to religious services all her life and tried to live up to what she thought her religion asked of her. She held the principles of kindness, compassion, and generosity close to her, but still, her husband, Edward, died of cancer as a young man.

"It doesn't make any sense. If there is a God, why would he take my husband away from me? When he became sick, I prayed and prayed, but in spite of that, he just got worse and died."

Annie doesn't attend services now. It seems pointless and ridiculous to her.

"I had never asked God for anything before. Finally, when I did ask, God wasn't listening."

Annie's feelings are common. Most of us remember times in our lives when things have gone badly and we attempted to make a deal with God. You know the way it goes: "If God gets me through this, then I'll give up smoking, or drinking, or gambling, or I'll give money to charity." Unfortunately, it doesn't seem to work that way. If there is anything that will cause you to question your beliefs or to question how the universe operates, it is having someone very close to you die. Your whole world turns upside down, and, after the shock is over, you may be missing parts of your life that you thought were very secure.

Some people hold their faith strong and fast through the death of someone they love. Some seem to have an even stronger faith afterwards. Other people develop rage and anger at God for taking their loved one away.

George lost any faith he had, and now he curses God for allowing a good woman like his wife, Win, to die a painful death at such a young age:

"Look at all the rotten people in the world: the killers, the cheaters, the people who hurt others.

So many of them seem to be doing fine – even
prospering. Yet my wife, who was kind and never
hurt anyone, is dead."

Sometimes it just seems that horrible things happen
to decent people. No one should talk you out of your
anger at God. Many of us have been taught since childhood to see God as a foolproof lifeguard who will always
be there to pull us out of the water. If that's what you've
been taught, then the anger that arises when you're let
down, especially when someone very close to you dies, is
completely understandable.

If you are angry with God, I encourage you to express
it. Some people are shocked when I suggest that. "How
could you ever get angry at God?" they ask me. My
answer is simple. If God is your friend and knows you
inside and out, then there shouldn't be anything that
you can't take to God. Certainly, there have been bibli-
cal examples of those who have been angry with God.
Job, Moses, and Jeremiah are three that quickly come
to mind.

This book is not the place to examine theology. It is
the place to help address feelings. There are far more
questions than there are answers. But to get beyond
your questions, your anger at God, and your rage over
injustices, you must deal with them.

Susan was unable to get beyond her grief because
she wasn't able to express her anger at God. She thought

she had an unspoken bargain with God. She believed she would be protected and helped whenever she needed it, as long as she was a "good" person. Until she could begin to say how hurt, betrayed, and angry she was that God had let her down, she couldn't gain any relief from her pain. If that sounds familiar, then I encourage you to express your feelings about God out loud. Find someone to listen to you without judgment.

If you have had a good relationship with a spouse or a friend, then you know that that relationship can grow only through mutual honesty. I think that it's meant to be that way with God too. You'll lose any relationship you have with God if you feel you can't be open and honest.

For Cathy, blowing up at God got some of her anger off her chest and allowed her to move on:

"I don't feel angry at God anymore. But if I hadn't expressed it, it would have choked me."

Many feel guilty when they question God. But life so often doesn't add up. Asking "Why him, God?" or "Why her, God? I don't understand, God!" is perfectly reasonable, even perfectly human.

I have seen many in grief use God and their faith in a most creative and helpful way to assist them, to help them get through this most painful time.

Linda has always had a strong faith in God. She reads her Bible regularly and has always had a strong sense of

God being present with her in her life. When her husband, Bob, died, she wasn't so sure:

> "At first I was angry, at life, at all those who dared to walk around and live it and enjoy it. Maybe I was even angry at God for leaving me in this mess with such loneliness and such emptiness. But then I remembered the things that I've always believed. I remembered that, although God's grace and love doesn't always make sense, I still believe it's there. I remembered that the things I've believed for so many years weren't so cheap and expendable that I could simply discard them when I needed them most. So I got out my Bible and I read passages that I've always felt were true. Except now I read them in a way that applied to me personally.
>
> "In the past, if I heard of other people dying, I would think, 'Oh, that's awful, but at least they're really with God now, no flesh and bones to separate them.' But now it's different. I need to find the strength to apply those thoughts and feelings to myself."

Linda's profound faith has been her rock of stability. She doesn't like what happened to her husband or to her life, but she has resigned herself to take comfort in the words and in the feelings that have touched her for years.

Kelly used prayer to help her through her miserable times:

> *"All my life I've thanked God for the good things around me. I've asked for help, strength, and courage to get through the tough times with the children, rough spots in our marriage, and concerns over people's health. I came to realize many years ago that God always hears our prayers. If we take the time to talk to God, God takes the time to listen. So when Glen died, I prayed even more. I prayed for the ability to go on believing that God was listening. I prayed to feel certain that Glen was with God. Even though I couldn't look after Glen anymore, I prayed that God would carry on where I could not. And you know, I believe it. Sure I need to, but I really believe that things are okay. I feel God's presence in my life, and I believe in my heart of hearts that Glen is okay."*

Prayer is a wonderful means of expression. I call it an authentic expression of life at the time. If life's good, reflect it in prayer; if it's not so good, take that to God in prayer too. The relationship we can have with God is like no other. So intimate, personal, revealing: nothing is hidden and nothing needs to be hidden. In the act of prayer we draw close, we become vulnerable and expose our needs, we open ourselves to be heard, and that in itself is very therapeutic.

Like Kelly, I have come to believe that God always answers prayers but not always in ways that we understand. Like Linda, I believe that God is present and a part of us in each breath we take. By coming to God with our hurts, our needs, our fears, and our worries, we draw close to the Divine. In that we can feel a healing and a wholeness like no other experience.

Children run to their parents when they are hurt. They don't necessarily expect the parent to fix their hurt, but they hope to gain a peace and a sense of warmth by asking for help and coming together. I believe prayer is a lot like that. It's a release, a drawing close, a feeling near, a sense of being heard – and, in that, of being helped.

We have become much more of an agnostic society. This may be one of the reasons why we have such a difficult time saying goodbye and letting go. We've learned to live merely for the here and now, and, for many, when there is no here and now, there is nothing but emptiness and despair.

I will not preach to you, but I will encourage you to take your anger to God. Likewise, if you have ever received hope, strength, or courage from God or your faith, you may draw on these comforts again when you are in the midst of death and loneliness.

No God

There are some people who go through grief without the added support of any kind of personal faith or organized religion. It is my experience that people who grieve, like Jennifer, remain consistent in their beliefs:

"All my life I've managed without believing in God. Now, I'll just have to go on coping with that position. My father-in-law died a few years ago and my mother-in-law really seemed to be helped by her religious point of view. She believed that her husband had gone to heaven to be with God. As for me, I believe only in the here and now. My husband, Randy, is gone from me forever. I can't

focus on an afterlife, but rather on all the good times we had, and all the good things we shared when he was alive."

People need to be consistent and true to themselves. If you have lived with no religious belief or personal conviction, then I strongly recommend that you carry on with the supports that you are used to.

Most of us have a network of support for when times are tough that may consist of our family members, close friends, a few people from work or a club we belong to. For a person with faith, it may also consist of his or her religious community or organization, or the clergy, and God.

If you do not have a religious faith, then you're not missing anything by not believing in God. You're not used to that resource and it would be foreign and inconsistent for you to try to use it during your grieving. There will be people who will be quite certain that, if you could only find God, you would have help and be guided through the pain that you are in. However, I would caution you to beware of quick fixes. What's helpful for one person may not be helpful for another, especially if you're not used to it or can't understand it. Alan recalls such a situation well:

"I know that people mean well, but hearing things about prayer and God has begun to drive me crazy, not help me cope with Barbara's death. For

a long time my 'church' has been the golf club. I've had some very special friends there for some time, and that's where I would go for support. I have always been anti-church and never believed in God. Barbara's death certainly wasn't a time for me to run to the church for help. If anything I wanted to shake my fists at it and everything else."

Alan's point is well taken. This is a time for him to rely on things that have worked for him in the past. This is a time for him to be consistent and to depend on what he knows will be helpful to him now.

If religion or faith has played no part in your life or has not been of help in times of need, then seek out those supports that have been helpful to you in the past. For Alan it was the golf club. For others it may be special friends or close family members. It's not a good time to be looking for substitute sources of help.

If a child is sad or frightened and is calling out for his or her mother or father, having another adult substitute for the parent is often of little or no use at all. The child needs to be with someone who is familiar, from whom he or she will get peace and comfort. When you're grieving, it's not much different. You must rely on what you know and understand to be helpful and useful to you.

Saying Goodbye

Experience tells me that, besides some of the fundamental difficulties that are common to people in grief, saying goodbye to the one who has died and visiting cemeteries can pose significant problems for many.

We all form strong bonds with those we love, so much so that saying goodbye can be very difficult. Whenever I'm involved with a death in the hospital, I always invite those in attendance to spend a few minutes with the body before it slips through the hospital and funeral home system. That time provides them with the opportunity to start to understand that their loved one has in fact died. It's the first goodbye, even if it lasts only for a few minutes.

Not all people take advantage of this opportunity, but many do. Some even stay and participate in the preparation and wrapping of the body for its send-off. Those few moments can be some of the most intimate and most important in the relationship. Touching, hugging, kissing, and speaking words that need to be said can be very therapeutic as the grief process begins. If these things don't happen then, there may never be the same chance again.

In our society the dead are often quickly taken to hospital morgues and then to funeral homes where they are prepared for burial or cremation. During this process, it may be very difficult for those left behind to have a moment of closeness – to do or say what they need to.

Many people have a hard time with this intimate contact with the dead body. I've seen family members and medical staff try to discourage this "last meeting." They prefer to hurry away those who are closest, thinking that there's something distasteful about being around a dead body. In fact, it can be very dangerous for us to impose our fears on those who are grieving. Those closest must have the opportunity to say goodbye in the manner they desire. If this isn't allowed to occur, their grieving may be delayed, and they may later feel cheated of an important experience.

How we say goodbye affects our relationship with cemeteries. There are two extremes in visiting cemeteries. Many people never visit the cemetery at all. If you've been able to do your parting business and say goodbye, you may never need to go to the cemetery. For others, it's as though there is something evil in the cemetery that must be avoided. If you haven't said goodbye to your loved one, and you avoid the cemetery because it's too painful, then you may need to make the effort to go and say farewell in spite of your fears.

Rina never goes near the cemetery. It gives her the creeps:

> *"I don't know what to do. I think of what's happened to Don's body over time and I'd rather think of him alive."*

She may very well need to get over her fear.

Others, in contrast, practically move into the cemetery. Wendy visits Dave's grave at least three times a week. Some weeks she goes more often than that. She simply can't let go because she still hasn't been able to say goodbye after more than two years.

Wendy tells me it feels good to be close to Dave at the cemetery as she feels a special sense of his presence there. I've encouraged her to feel that presence wherever she is. If, as Wendy believes, Dave's spirit survived the death of his body, then his presence can accompany her wherever she is.

Peter went three or four times to the cemetery where his wife Elizabeth is buried. Each time he felt very sad and weepy:

"It was driving me crazy. I felt I needed to be there, but I knew there was nothing there for me. After several months, when I finally felt strong enough, I returned to her grave to bid her farewell."

Doing this allowed Peter to start to rebuild his life.

Louise's husband, Keith, was a Christmas person. For all the years she had known him, he loved the special feeling of the warmth and giving that goes along with Christmas. He would put up the family Christmas tree in mid-November, attempting to create that warm feeling as early as he could manage it.

Since his death, Louise visits Keith's grave at Christmastime with their children and grandchildren. They erect a small decorated Christmas tree by the grave. It gives them a chance to remember something warm and special.

"I don't feel I need to go to the cemetery. I said good-bye some time ago. But this seems like a nice way to remember, and I think Keith would approve."

Whatever we do, we must say goodbye before we can get on with our lives. Parting with someone you love is terribly painful. We have a need to keep him or her near to us at all costs. Never going to the cemetery, or, alternatively, camping there, will not accomplish that. A photo may be a more suitable substitute to remember them by. Those we love remain with us indelibly forever in our hearts, our memories, and our being. Nothing can change that. However, before we can get on with our lives without the one who has died, we must find a way to say goodbye. If there has been time, some are successful at saying goodbye before the death. Others begin to say goodbye at the time of death. Still others, like Peter, must do it when they are ready, over a long period of time.

Don't let anyone force you to say goodbye in a particular way. We do things when we are ready. However, you must remember that, until you find a way to say goodbye, you will have trouble letting go, healing, and getting on with your life.

How Do I Grieve?

Throughout this book I have been urging you to deal with your grief by expressing yourself, by talking things through, and by finding a way to do what your feelings encourage you to do. That's easy for me to say, but I remember that not so long ago I didn't have any idea what it meant to share or express my own feelings. I have had people teach me how to express myself, so let me illustrate some of that for you.

The simplest way for you to learn how to express your grief is to find someone who will listen and encourage you to describe how you are feeling, and who will not be judgmental or try to talk you out of whatever you feel. If possible, find someone who is used to helping people deal with grief and who does so on a regular basis.

Your family doctor, local hospital, or social services agency should be able to recommend someone who is skilled in grief counselling. Expect the counsellor to ask you open-ended questions that you will be able to respond to at length. They might include:

- Tell me about the person who has died.
- Tell me about your relationship.
- What's it like to be without your loved one?
- What's an average day like for you?
- How's your eating? Your sleeping? Your energy?
- Do you find yourself crying a lot?
- What are the strongest feelings you have?
- What thoughts make you cry?

Over time, as you develop a trusting relationship, your helper should be able to assist you with expressing yourself. By expressing your feelings, you will eventually find some relief from your pain.

Though groups are unfortunately not available in all communities, if there is one in yours it may be worth seeking out. A group can provide you with a safe, permissive place where you can be around people who have also lost a loved one. Walter tells me that our bereavement group is one of the highlights of his week:

*"It's a place where I can be honest. No one judges
me. No one tells me what I should or shouldn't feel."*

If there are no groups or professional counsellors
available in your community, a couple of other options
are open to you. You could ask a close friend or family
member to help you explore your feelings. You will need
to choose someone who is a good listener – someone
who can be empathetic and patient with you, and who
is able to hear your sadness, anger, or fear, or whatever
your feelings may be.

Writing can also be a useful tool. If there is no one
to talk to, many people find it very helpful to express
themselves on paper. Make notes from time to time, or
maintain a daily journal so that you have a regular opportunity to write about your emotions. The benefit of
writing is that paper will never contradict you. A draw-
back is that paper will provide no empathy for you.

Sandra found that writing was foreign to her, but she
felt that she was not the kind of person who could easily
share with others, so she bought herself a tape recorder
and recorded her daily journal:

*"I would even play the tapes back later. It was a
great way to see what bridges I had crossed, what
progress I had made. Sometimes listening to the
tapes made me very sad. But in time they showed
me I was really beginning to feel better."*

All of these methods of grief work allow you to express your feelings. The method is not important, only the process, which will, in time, allow you to come to some sort of resolution about your feelings. I strongly believe that if painful feelings stay bottled up inside you, sooner or later they will come back to haunt you.

Martin, a young man, came to see me some time ago. His mother died when he was a child. He came to me with what he called "things undone":

> "Ever since my mother died, I've never cried. I've never said how much I hurt; I've just gotten on with my life. But now that I am a man, I know I have missed something. I carry all this emotional burden around inside me, and, as I get older, I get angrier and more foul-tempered. It is really getting to be a problem for me. I am sure it is all connected to my unresolved grief over my mother's death."

Monica and Lloyd were both admitted to the hospital many months after their spouses had died. Everyone believed that they had suffered heart attacks. In fact, they had not had heart attacks, and both were told that their symptoms probably had to do with the huge stresses that they were carrying around with them.

Monica remembers how her unresolved grief finally exploded:

"I had gone straight back to work. Every time I felt a void, I just worked harder and longer. Then after almost a year I had my 'heart attack.' When I came out of the hospital, I was an emotional mess. I spent all my time crying. Now, a year later and after much work, I feel alive again. I haven't had to avoid my feelings. I faced them and finally dealt with them."

Lloyd finally went to his best friend and asked for help:

"He's been fantastic. He listens to me. He lets me cry. He understands if I need to leave suddenly. At times, he even weeps with me. What a relief to know that I don't have to hide my feelings or be strong in front of everyone any longer."

A grief group, a grief counsellor, a good friend, a journal – any one, all, or a combination of these are designed to give you permission to feel as you need to. Once you accept the fact that you have been through a major emotional trauma that has had an effect on how you feel and act, then you will allow yourself permission to express and work through your grief.

If you have had open-heart surgery, you and everyone around you gives you permission to go slowly, to say ouch, and to take the time you need to heal yourself. In grief, the emotional wounds are even more severe. You must take the time to work at healing them.

Learning to Live
Without Your Loved One

A s Benjamin sat with me this morning, I watched his painful body language, saw his tears, and listened to the nightmare-like story of his young wife's illness and death.

"She's been dead almost five weeks and I'm no better. Sometimes I feel worse than I did before. Is this going to end soon?"

With all my heart, I wanted to say, "Yes, you'll be a new man and a healed man in a few days." However, I could only commiserate and tell him some of the things that I have told you: "This pain, this terrible roller coaster that you're on, will likely go on for a long time to come, but take heart. As you acknowledge your painful feelings you will work through this terrible time."

"I can't tell you how much fear I have. Fear of tomorrow and whether I'll get through it. Fear of the future and whether I'll have one myself. Most of all, I fear being alone and I hate how awful my reality is.

"It's funny, isn't it? My wife tried so hard to hold on to life, to cling to some kind of tomorrow. She begged, pleaded, and prayed to be allowed to live, even for another day! Me, I feel like I'd rather be dead. My whole world is gone. There's nothing to live for or to look forward to."

Ben's words were so powerful that they moved me. I went on to explain that he needed to take time to be a mess. His whole world had been turned upside down, and he would need to pause to assess what that meant for him. "Give yourself permission," I urged, "permission to feel sad, lonely, empty, angry, and helpless. There may never be a time in your life when you feel so helpless, so powerless. You have just watched your loved one die, and there was little, if anything, you could do about it. You've watched your hopes, your plans, and your dreams, die with her. None of it has been within your control. You are now left with a life that seems to have little or no meaning, direction, or worth. As you work through your grief, don't forget some of the changes that you may experience – changes in your appetite, your sleep pattern, your motivation and energy, and your mood. Remember that anger may be a problem for you over the first several months of your grief. It often gets directed all over the place, to friends and family, especially when you least expect it. If you have a relationship with God, don't be surprised if your anger is directed toward your faith. Don't be too quick to believe that all of these new feelings and questions will be with you forever. Give them some time. Work at them. You will likely stabilize in the future.

"However you feel, whatever you do, give yourself permission to take all of these feelings and changes in, and act accordingly. Cry if you're sad, yell if you're angry, and sit quietly in the corner if you've lost your bearings. Tell someone how you feel when the pain becomes so great that you need to express it. They cannot read your mind and will need your help to understand what's happening to you before they can respond. Don't try to suppress your pain, or it will only go deep inside and rattle around, causing you harm."

I briefly laid out the three Rs for Benjamin. I doubt he heard very much, so we'll simply plod along over the weeks and months ahead, gradually sorting them out.

"Realize that Deborah has died. Then, realize the pain that goes along with the knowledge that Deborah has died. That will hurt."

"It couldn't hurt any more than it does now. All I seem to be able to do is cry. She had this old wool sweater that she loved. Sometimes she even wore it in the summer, she enjoyed it so much. At night I just bury my face in it and weep. Am I crazy?"

I simply shook my head, thinking it sounded pretty sane to me.

"After you realize what has happened, the longest, and maybe the hardest part of all is recognizing the significance of Deborah's death. Take the time to know what your wife's death will do to your life, your hopes and plans, your dreams and your daily routine."

"Every night we would walk in the park, come rain or shine – even in the snow. I couldn't sleep properly if we didn't go for a walk in that park. Now, I can't even look at it. It makes me feel sick!"

That may very well be how Benjamin will feel on some of the special days that he will be facing alone over the next year: Deborah's birthday, Christmas, their wedding anniversary. These and other times that were special for him are likely to cause him anger, pain, and a deep, empty sickness that he will find difficult to deal with.

"In time, things will change as you work at your feelings. The ugly, haunting memories will fade, and you will begin to remember Deborah as she was in good times. In time, your wounds will heal and you will permit yourself to say goodbye and begin to rebuild your life without her."

Sarah Duncan and I said goodbye after we had been together for just over a year. Few stones had been left unturned. Now, she doesn't cry as much. She doesn't feel as sad or lonely. She's beginning to look to the future with a sense of hope.

Initially Sarah simply couldn't believe what had happened. "I know it's a bad dream," she would say to me. "I just wish I'd get to the waking-up part." Then, for a long time she just felt the pain of her loss and simply cried. From there we spent months looking at how the death of her husband would dramatically and permanently affect her life.

My role as caregiver has been to commiserate with her, to provide her with a safe, secure, permissive place where she could say what she needed to, without judgment, without manipulation, without trying to talk her into or out of her feelings. That can be difficult to do at times. I often need to remind myself that feelings have no moral value. They simply are, and they need to be expressed and recognized.

I've given you an overview of some grief reactions that I have come to recognize as typical. That's not to say they've all been explored, but I've touched upon many of them. I've given you some sense of what healthy and unhealthy grief look like, and I encourage you to find someone with whom you feel safe, to say and feel what you need to. That person may be able to alert you to grief reactions that are becoming unhealthy.

When someone you love dies, your world is changed forever. That does not mean that things will never be good again. I wish I could tell you there was a quick and easy way through all of this, but it doesn't exist. With hard work, grief can be managed; life can have new meaning and new worth. You will learn to live without your loved one. As Peter said when he visited Elizabeth's grave:

"Goodbye, my friend, my love. I don't love you any less. I still care deeply for you, but from here I go alone."

Notes

Notes

Resources

The following is a list of websites that may be helpful to you.

Those who live in or near large cities are likely to have access to more resources and services, but even in small communities, your hospital, hospice, palliative care services, family doctor, or local funeral services may be able to put you in touch with a group or an individual who may be able to help.

Depending on the circumstances surrounding the death of the person that you are grieving, you may have very specific needs. For example, a death from suicide may require a different response than a death from terminal illness. The death of a child may need a different kind of response than the death of a friend.

Suggested Places to Begin Your Search

In Canada:
Bereaved Families of Ontario – Toronto
WWW.BFOTORONTO.CA

Canadian Hospice Palliative Care Association
WWW.CHPCA.NET

Canadian Mental Health Association

WWW.CMHA.CA/MENTAL_HEALTH/GRIEVING
/#.UCLMK46ABDK

Canadian Network of Palliative Care for Children

WWW.CNPCC.CA

Canadian Virtual Hospice

WWW.VIRTUALHOSPICE.CA

In the U.S.:

International Palliative Care Resource Center

WWW.IPCRC.NET

National Hospice and Palliative Care Organization

WWW.NHPCO.ORG